social distance sing

pandemic poems

social distance sing
pandemic poems

april 1 – april 30, 2020

steve potter

For First Responders Everywhere

PREFACE

The title of this book was inspired by the videos of Italians in quarantine singing from their balconies that circulated around social media in mid-March while Italy was on lock-down to help stem the rising tide of the COVID 19 coronavirus outbreak that was devastating that country.

As of the date of this writing, according to the website worldometers.info, the COVID 19 strain of the coronavirus is confirmed to have infected 3,810,709 people and killed at least 264,020 worldwide. Tracking the rise of the virus became a part of this book as the writing process went along. All of the statistics which appear herein are from the Worldometers site.

Those confirmed numbers are certainly lower than the actual numbers. Many people found dead in their homes in New York City, for example, have not been autopsied to determine if the virus was a factor in their death and, therefore, are not included in those "confirmed" numbers. Likely, many of them would have been if autopsies had been performed. We know that the rate of testing here in the US has been woefully inadequate and now, right as people are becoming so itchy to get back to "normal" that armed protesters have stormed the capitol in Michigan and gathered in other states as well, it appears that we have not even reached the peak of the first wave of the virus.

According to a recent *New York Times* article, a study by the Institute for Health Metrics and Evaluation at the University of Washington here in Seattle estimates up to 135,000 deaths in the US by early August, more than double their earlier prediction on April 17th of 60,308 deaths by August 4th. That number has already been surpassed well over two months earlier than predicted. The number of confirmed US deaths as of today is

social distance sing

74,121.

My mantra lately has been "stop starting and finish." I've been writing nearly every day for almost forty years and the projects-in-progress have piled up. I've always chosen to emphasize writing in my free time after work and on the weekends more so than spending time sending work out to seek recognition. It's a pastime I do for enjoyment, not a career. I'm not in the game, I'm off to the side but eventual publication was always part of the plan. Now I'm getting old. I'm running out of time. I could die of the 'rona any day now! I should be finishing the old projects and releasing them one way or another, not beginning new projects.

So how did I wind up writing something new instead? On April Fool's Day, I saw a Facebook thread of poets writing "quarantine haiku" and (foolishly or not) joined in. "Pandemic poetry" was (as one might have expected) becoming a *thing*. I wrote a couple more on April 3rd and a bunch on the 4th.

What I (and most of the other "quarantine haiku" poets in that initial thread) were writing would really be better classified as that close cousin of haiku, senryu. The snapshot-like brevity of senryu (or, more accurately still, English language approximation of senryu) felt right to me in our current period of uncertainty caused by decades of sociopolitical deterioration exacerbated and dragged into the light by the global coronavirus pandemic.

I decided that for the remainder of the month I would take a little time each day to think in short poetic forms about our current situation. Poetic *form* is really kind of a misnomer. Poetic *pattern* is more accurate, and a poetic pattern is first and foremost a mode of thought. While most of what I wrote was English language approximation of senryu, haiku or tanka, the scope expanded beyond that to include a variety of other shorties such as acrostics, cinquains, limericks, naani, nonets, and one triolet. Other little blips of consciousness I included – sometimes aphoristic, sometimes impressionistic – don't fit under any of those classifications. Blips. I just think of them as little mind blips.

I opted for more of a "ragged glory" daily journal presentation than a polished "greatest hits" style poetry collection, so I've resisted the impulse to rearrange the poems (and mind blips) for greater impact. With a few exceptions, they are presented here in the order in which they were written. The exceptions fall into two categories.

During the writing process, I moved a few poems written later in the month up in the book. These were poems inspired by, and clearly related to, one of the earlier poems. If a later poem sat more comfortably behind the earlier poem that inspired it, in terms of the flow of the manuscript as a whole, I moved it forward.

The other category of moved poems are those I flipped the order of while formatting the final layout for the book so as to eliminate any big blank spaces on the pages. Most of the poems are three-to-five lines long and arranged three to a page, but the longest pattern used – nonets – are nine lines. In a few cases I changed the order and put two long(ish) poems on a page rather than one long and one short and a blank space.

The nation and the world seem to be careening toward some kind of a breaking point. That was the case even before the virus came along to exacerbate the situation and highlight the deep unfairness, inequality, and cruelty of our world. Buckle up and hold on tight. Things are likely to get even weirder and uglier and sadder in the coming months.

social distance sing

Yesterday, Governor Inslee extended the stay-at-home order through, at least, May 31st here in Washington State. The pandemic has slowed our hyperkinetic world to a sloth's pace. Like an overstimulated hyperactive child taken from an overcrowded classroom and taught to meditate, the world has been forced to slow down and take a look at itself. It's awful. It's wonderful. I hate it. I love it.

We should slow down. We need to change our ways. The voracious materialistic appetite of the industrialized world for more and more stuff is unsustainable. We shouldn't need a global pandemic to recognize that the way we are living and the way our society is organized is quite insane and has been for many years. It is difficult for anyone who is paying even the slightest bit of attention to be optimistic these days, but maybe this pandemic is what we need. Maybe it will force us to finally recognize, as Otis Redding put it so many years ago, "a change has gotta come."

Seattle, Washington, May 6th, 2020

social distance sing

i travel to such
beautiful landscapes eyes closed
sitting in my chair

april 1st, 2020

intensely he washed
his hands with soap and water
afraid he'd touched death

april 3rd, 2020

life now is so small
a trip down to the mailbox
the day's big event

april 3rd, 2020

social distance sing

big gang of young men
fist fight beneath the footbridge
social distance fail

april 4th, 2020, 2:16 a.m. p.s.t.

"going out" now means
i stick my head out window
look this way and that

april 4th, 2020, 2:19 a.m. p.s.t.

to mask or not to mask
that is the question with
no clear answer yet

april 4th, 2020, 2:47 a.m. p.s.t.

social distance sing

during pandemic
social distancing is key
to stopping the spread

april 4th, 2020, 10:57 a.m. p.s.t.

the whole world's been forced
into monasticism
for the good of all

april 4th, 2020, 10:59 a.m. p.s.t.

on the high school track
people walk in slow circles
keeping six feet apart

april 4th, 2020, 11:11 a.m. p.s.t.

social distance sing

isn't it strange when
the invisible world makes
itself known to us

april, 4ᵗʰ, 11:12 a.m. p.s.t.

isn't it strange how
some religious people won't
listen to science

april 4ᵗʰ, 2020, 11:14 a.m. p.s.t.

isn't it sad that
people will die because
they wouldn't listen

april 4ᵗʰ, 2020, 11:16 a.m. p.s.t.

social distance sing

isn't it tragic
that people will die because
others wouldn't listen

april 4ᵗʰ, 2020, 11:17 a.m. p.s.t.

it is said that god
protects fools and children but
it's not always true

april 4ᵗʰ, 2020, 11:18 a.m. p.s.t.

every single day
an aging idol reported
sickened or dead

april 4ᵗʰ, 2020, 1:06 p.m. p.s.t.

social distance sing

"believe none of what
you hear and half of what you
see" leads to death now

april 4th, 2020, 1:16 p.m. p.s.t.

so sad so sad
sister morphine make up her bed
as tears go by

(hoping for the best for marianne faithfull)
april 4th, 2020, 1:36 p.m. p.s.t.

outdated views of
invisible agency
lead to early death

april 4th, 2020, 1:39 p.m. p.s.t.

social distance sing

god may hear your prayers
but the deadly virus is deaf
doctors before priests

april 4th, 2020, 1:42 p.m. p.s.t.

many dreams to chase
unfinished plans to complete
death doesn't care

april 4th, 2020, 8:01 p.m. p.s.t.

moderates call
health care for all "pie in the sky"
during pandemic

april 4th, 2020, 9:51 p.m. p.s.t.

social distance sing

remember that line
"i *am* in a world of shit"
from *full metal jacket*

april 4th, 2020, 9:51 p.m. p.s.t.

how much more abuse
will we take before we break
working people

april 4th, 2020, 9:55 p.m. p.s.t.

will the class war soon
go from cold to boiling hot
will the workers win

april 4th, 2020, 10:02 p.m. p.s.t.

are you in my room
now invisible killer
are you in my lungs

april 4th, 2020, 10:11 p.m. p.s.t.

what is "moderate"
about indifference to
human suffering

april 4th, 2020, 10:20 p.m. p.s.t.

what is "centrist"
about indifference
to human suffering

april 4th, 2020, 10:23 p.m. p.s.t.

why not say "greedist"
why not say "inhumanist"
why not be honest

april 4th, 2020, 10:25 p.m. p.s.t.

sirens wail outside
cops at arco gas station
lights flashing red blue

april 4th, 2020, 10:52 p.m. p.s.t.

sirens sirens sirens
cop cars race south down rainier
never ends down here

april 4th, 2020, 10:55 p.m. p.s.t.

social distance sing

head out the window
virus breeze through my gray beard
today just tomorrowed

april 5th, 2020, 12:03 a.m. p.s.t.

traffic light turns red
traffic light turns green two cars
traffic light turns red

april 5th, 2020 1:29 a.m. p.s.t.

sixty-four-thousand-
seven-hundred-forty-eight
confirmed deaths to date

april 5th, 2020 1:32 a.m. p.s.t.

21

social distance sing

"you down with cdc"
"yeah you know me"
"you down with cdc"
"yeah you know me"

april 5th, 2020 1:36 a.m. p.s.t.

first cup of coffee
plan the day's top writing goals
then get on with it

april 5th, 2020, 7:13 a.m. p.s.t.

the president is
a sociopathic liar
getting people killed

april 5th, 2020, 10:32 a.m. p.s.t.

social distance sing

many christian preachers
are sociopathic liars
getting people killed

april 5th, 2020, 10:34 a.m. p.s.t.

conflicting advice
from legitimate sources
wear mask don't wear mask

april 5th, 2020, 2:09 p.m. p.s.t.

a cough or a sneeze
carries the virus so stay
six feet away

april 5th, 2020, 10:34 a.m. p.s.t.

social distance sing

no not enough now
some say stay twenty-seven
feet away stay home

april 5th, 2020, 2:12 p.m. p.s.t.

six feet away is
ninety-year-old advice
death rides a mere breath

april 5th, 2020, 2:15 p.m. p.s.t.

yes death rides mere breath
no need for a cough or sneeze
so wear a mask please

april 5th, 2020, 2:17 p.m. p.s.t.

social distance sing

a mask are you sure
some say so but some say no
stay indoors alone

april 5th, 2020, 2:19 p.m. p.s.t.

we introverts
we're suited to isolation
read write meditate

april 5th, 2020, 3:30 p.m. p.s.t.

out the window
the world continues to look
quite busy slow down

april 5th, 2020, 3:31 p.m. p.s.t.

social distance sing

some say change will come
on the heels of pandemic
i don't believe it

april 5th, 2020, 3:34 p.m. p.s.t.

avarice and greed
are alive and well no change
hoarding price gouging

april 5th, 2020, 3:35 p.m. p.s.t.

gun sales skyrocket
churches continue services
pray shoot the virus

april 5th, 2020, 3:46 p.m. p.s.t.

how difficult is it
to understand how this works
just stay home simple

april 5th, 2020, 3:48 p.m. p.s.t.

how are the homeless
expected to stay at home
without having homes

april 5th, 2020, 3:49 p.m. p.s.t.

how are the working poor
expected to pay rent
without being paid

april 5th, 2020, 3:50 p.m. p.s.t.

social distance sing

the reprehensible
cruelty of daily life
is being exposed

april 5th, 2020, 3:52 p.m. p.s.t.

what's accepted as
normal is untenable
we must change our ways

april 5th, 2020, 4:44 p.m. p.s.t.

outside two crows fly
side by side sleek black crosses
on a deep gray sky

april 5th, 2020, 4:51 p.m. p.s.t.

social distance sing

men on the sidewalk
walk then stop and stand and talk
wave and walk away

april 5th, 2020, 4:53 p.m. p.s.t.

the bus arrives
no one enters no one leaves
the bus departs

april 5th, 2020, 4:54 p.m. p.s.t.

another day come and gone
dark and quiet now
empty parking lot

april 6th, 2020, 12:08 a.m. p.s.t.

social distance sing

nearly silent now
tree limbs white in street light's glow
distant car engine revs

april 6th, 2020, 12:10 a.m. p.s.t.

social dis dancing
punk rock mosh pit way back when
"and there's no future"

april 6th, 2020, 12:13 a.m. p.s.t.

"god save the queen"
sang johnny rotten snide and
dripping with disdain

april 6th, 2020, 12:23 a.m. p.s.t.

30

social distance sing

take me back to when
"sheena is a punk rocker"
was brand new and fresh

april 6th, 2020, 12:26 a.m. p.s.t.

oh take me back please
I wanna be sedated
dancing to ramones

april 6th, 2020, 12:26 a.m. p.s.t.

what is the point of
this crazy human body trip
cradle to grave

april 6th, 2020, 12:35 a.m. p.s.t.

social distance sing

we are here to dance
we are here to laugh and sing
we are here to love

april 6th, 2020, 12:41 a.m. p.s.t.

"dance this mess around"
"dance me to the end of love"
"dancing in the dark"

april 6th, 2020, 12:56 a.m. p.s.t.

the virus spreads from
person to person to person
no dancing for now

april 6th, 2020, 2:12 a.m. p.s.t.

social distance sing

no dancing in nightclubs
no drinking in taverns
no out on the town

april 6ᵗʰ, 2020, 2:14 a.m. p.s.t.

covid 19 has
now infected a tiger
in the bronx zoo

april 6ᵗʰ, 2020, 2:16 a.m. p.s.t.

is the earth dying
or is it being reborn
is there a difference

april 6ᵗʰ, 2020, 12:56 a.m. p.s.t.

33

social distance sing

silent as a stone
i sit content and at peace
in my small room alone

april 6th, 2020, 2:34 a.m. p.s.t.

happiness is not
on a store shelf to be bought
sit still go within

april 6th, 2020, 2:37 a.m. p.s.t.

red lights on radio towers pulse
hearts beating in the dark night sky

april 6th, 2020, 2:42 a.m. p.s.t.

social distance sing

hot bath and ideas flow forth
new poems new stories
lyrics for songs

april 6th, 2020, 11:17 a.m. p.s.t.

cup of coffee
new day
new possibilities
stare at the sky
think

april 6th, 2020, 11:40 p.m. p.s.t.

busybodies
out and about below
I glare down
from four floors up

april 6th, 2020, 12:56 p.m. p.s.t.

social distance sing

what part of the word
"essential"
don't you get
stay home
stay home
stay home

april 6th, 2020, 12:58 p.m. p.s.t.

flowers in bloom
and people in masks outside
springtime pandemic

april 6th, 2020, 2:30 p.m. p.s.t.

seventy-four-thousand-
five-hundred-twenty-two
confirmed deaths to date

april 6th, 2020 3:36 p.m. p.s.t.

social distance sing

corporate con-men
guests on nightly network news
always an agenda

april 6th, 2020 6:46 p.m. p.s.t.

they talk and they talk
but speak not a word of truth
lying for profit

april 6th, 2020 6:50 p.m. p.s.t.

please stay safe out there
death is in the air tonight
masked men everywhere

april 6th, 2020 8:35 p.m. p.s.t.

social distance sing

kakistocracy
we're led by fools and madmen
now it's costing lives

april 6th, 2020 11:26 p.m. p.s.t.

kleptocracy
we're led by thieves and conmen
scamming for a buck

april 6th, 2020 11:28 p.m. p.s.t.

coronavirus
killing tens of thousands
rich men get richer

april 7th, 2020 3:40 a.m. p.s.t.

social distance sing

eighty-one-thousand-
forty-nine confirmed
deaths to date

april 7th, 2020 11:42 p.m. p.s.t.

avaricious swine
corporate snouts in government trough
workers in food bank lines

april 7th, 2020 1:14 p.m. p.s.t.

trillion plus dollar
corporate bailout but no masks
for hospital nurses

april 7th, 2020 1:16 p.m. p.s.t.

social distance sing

john prine put it well
"that's how every empire falls"
get well kind sir

april 7th, 2020 1:19 p.m. p.s.t.

hairless ape
the rock you throw
aiming for the sun
comes down on your head

april 7th, 2020 1:33 p.m. p.s.t.

the results are in
ben franklin
and it's clear now
we'll hang separately

april 7th, 2020 1:35 p.m. p.s.t.

social distance sing

what a marvel is man
just joking
man is an
undeniable mess

april 7th, 2020 1:37 p.m. p.s.t.

sending hopes and prayers
to the sick and dying
won't help
send ventilators

april 7th, 2020 1:40 p.m. p.s.t.

what a marvel is man
just joking
man is a greedy beast
with murder on its mind

april 7th, 2020 1:42 p.m. p.s.t.

social distance sing

dreaming of space flight
trashing the one good planet
we're sure can stand us

april 7th, 2020 1:51 p.m. p.s.t.

talking out both sides
of their mouths
gang of grifters
in the capitol

april 7th, 2020 1:54 p.m. p.s.t.

many miles apart
we are alone together
connected online

april 7th, 2020 3:19 p.m. p.s.t.

social distance sing

what new world is this
we stand at the portal to
with our hopes and fears

april 7th, 2020 3:23 p.m. p.s.t.

pigeons on the roof
not a one of them hoarding
toilet paper

april 7th, 2020 5:18 p.m. p.s.t.

coronavirus
great teacher
toward what future
will your lessons lead

april 7th, 2020 5:18 p.m. p.s.t.

social distance sing

aw hell john prine
fishin' and whistlin'
in heaven

april 7th, 2020 8:49 p.m. p.s.t.

late capitalism
american upside
down cake blues

april 7th, 2020 9:11 p.m. p.s.t.

villains in the roles
heroes should play
heroes treated as villains

april 7th, 2020 9:11 p.m. p.s.t.

social distance sing

doctors die at work
cowards in the capitol
steal the silverware

april 7th, 2020 9:15 p.m. p.s.t.

bill withers john prine
duet in heaven tonight
chorus of angels

april 7th, 2020 10:56 p.m. p.s.t.

perhaps they'll include
a cover of nick drake's
"pink moon"

april 7th, 2020 11:00 p.m. p.s.t.

45

social distance sing

world's going through hell
old advice is "keep going"
dante virgil help

april 7th, 2020 11:31 p.m. p.s.t.

they're dreaming of fall
the trees are tired of us
they want us to leave

april 7th, 2020 11:00 p.m. p.s.t.

fascism on the rise
authoritarian rule
fools at the controls

april 8th, 2020 12:02 a.m. p.s.t.

social distance sing

withers gone prine gone
sanders out of the running
fuck life back to bed

april 8th, 2020, 8:47 a.m. p.s.t.

okay no
still awake back to work
onward onward

april 8th, 2020, 9:14 a.m. p.s.t.

novel to finish
poems to write
songs to write
someday looking back
what will be seen

april 8th, 2020, 9:16 a.m. p.s.t.

social distance sing

what poetry was
what poetry is
what poetry will become

april 8th, 2020, 9:31 a.m. p.s.t.

such disappointment life
perhaps a jaunt outside
to get sneezed on

april 8th, 2020, 11:15 a.m. p.s.t.

ionesco sartre beckett
not sure which but want
this play we're in to end

april 8th, 2020, 11:20 a.m. p.s.t.

social distance sing

eighty-seven-thousand-
six-hundred-seventeen confirmed
deaths to date

april 8th, 2020, 12:36 p.m. p.s.t.

one thing i'm sure of
i'm not sure of anything
of that i'm certain

april 8th, 2020, 2:21 p.m. p.s.t.

a better world is
possible just not probable
which yeah i know sucks

april 8th, 2020, 3:14 p.m. p.s.t.

social distance sing

i've been here before
at the bathroom sink soapy
hands beneath the tap

april 8th, 2020, 7:23 p.m. p.s.t.

i'm washing my hands
virus era deja vu
i'm washing my hands

april 8th, 2020, 7:30 p.m. p.s.t.

i'm touching my face
stop touching your face
stop it stop it
i'm touching my face

april 8th, 2020, 7:33 p.m. p.s.t.

social distance sing

i washed my hands so
it's okay to touch my face
because deja vu

april 8th, 2020, 7:35 p.m. p.s.t.

talking to myself
stop talking to yourself
you stop answering me

april 8th, 2020, 7:42 p.m. p.s.t.

not much good news but
at least those two pandas in
that zoo finally fucked

april 8th, 2020, 7:48 p.m. p.s.t.

social distance sing

i like to talk to you
which is good since you're me
we're together a lot

april 8th, 2020, 11:49 p.m. p.s.t.

i like you too me
we make a great team
all one of us two

april 8th, 2020, 11:53 p.m. p.s.t.

indeed what would i do without me
face it you'd be lost without you

april 8th, 2020, 11:56 p.m. p.s.t.

social distance sing

when this thing's over
i'll probably keep doing
the same stuff anyhow

april 8th, 2020, 11:58 p.m. p.s.t.

some of these poems
aren't very poemy
so sue me

april 8th, 2020, 11:59 p.m. p.s.t.

sew sumi paintings
together to make handbags
such lovely brushstrokes

april 9th, 2020, 12:02 a.m. p.s.t.

social distance sing

silly arrogant
pretentious deluded fools
such a joy to meet

april 9th, 2020, 10:42 a.m. p.s.t.

memories of morons
why have you invaded
my mind this morning

april 9th, 2020, 10:43 a.m. p.s.t.

hey think happy thoughts
it seems the curve's
been flattened
here in seattle

april 9th, 2020, 10:45 a.m. p.s.t.

social distance sing

lovely pale blue sky
nice day to catch a virus
sunshine and cool breeze

april 9th, 2020, 10:45 a.m. p.s.t.

fool in the white house
thieves head every cabinet
bernie has the conch

april 9th, 2020, 11:58 a.m. p.s.t.

divided states of
absurdistan collapsing
what shall be born

april 9th, 2020, 12:01 p.m. p.s.t.

social distance sing

honey bucket truck
in u s bank parking lot
they're both full of it

april 9th, 2020, 12:05 a.m. p.s.t.

tens of millions of
newly unemployed workers
no sign of relief

april 9th, 2020, 1:09 a.m. p.s.t.

ninety-three-thousand-
four-hundred-twenty-five confirmed
deaths to date

april 9th, 2020, 1:13 p.m. p.s.t.

social distance sing

faint smile tear-streaked cheeks
old eyes gazing at the world
dreams castles ruins

april 10th, 2020, 12:05 a.m. p.s.t.

the biggest office
on the highest floor
he stares down
completely lost

april 10th, 2020, 12:14 a.m. p.s.t.

listening to old songs
memories swim through like fish
what was her name

april 10th, 2020, 12:22 a.m. p.s.t.

social distance sing

transported hearing
janis sing "at seventeen"
"society's child"

april 10th, 2020, 12:25 a.m. p.s.t.

"i've looked at love from
both sides now" joni mitchell
and clouds... also clouds

april 10th, 2020, 12:29 a.m. p.s.t.

bob dylan singing
"visions of johanna" and
his conscience explodes

april 10th, 2020, 12:32 a.m. p.s.t.

social distance sing

mass grave in new york
dozens of white pine caskets
in one long brown ditch

april 10th, 2020, 1:19 a.m. p.s.t.

empty coffee shop
chairs flipped up on table tops
no music lights out

april 10th, 2020, 7:31 a.m. p.s.t.

boarded up storefronts
downtown streets vacant quiet
empty shopping cart

april 10th, 2020, 7:35 a.m. p.s.t.

social distance sing

before corona
you are here x marks the spot
after corona

april 10ʰ, 2020, 8:26 a.m. p.s.t.

new ghost stories born
in this time of infection
listen to the wind

april 10ʰ, 2020, 8:31 a.m. p.s.t.

no sounds in the hall
where have all the neighbors gone
let's make zombie jokes

april 10ʰ, 2020, 12:20 p.m. p.s.t.

social distance sing

one-hundred-one-thousand-
seven-hundred-sixty-two
confirmed deaths to date

april 10th, 2020, 12:25 p.m. p.s.t.

angry man shouting
hum of car traffic
lone horn
somewhere someone died

april 10th, 2020, 12:28 p.m. p.s.t.

washington dc
a smiling politician
eats a golden cookie

april 10th, 2020, 12:34 p.m. p.s.t.

social distance sing

minor slights add up
insults and indignities
seeds of holocaust

april 11th, 2020, 10:41 a.m. p.s.t.

sit alone and stare
slow-drifting gray morning clouds
world ripe with new ghosts

april 11th, 2020, 10:41 a.m. p.s.t.

one-hundred-seven-
thousand-seven-hundred-fifteen
confirmed deaths to date

april 11th, 2020, 11:34 a.m. p.s.t.

social distance sing

nostalgia trip day
fifties rock 'n' roll classics
let's go to the hop

april 11ᵗʰ, 2020, 11:52 a.m. p.s.t.

who i was is not
who i am is not who i'll
be eventually

april 11ᵗʰ, 2020, 11:55 a.m. p.s.t.

old enduring snake
how many skins have you shed
in this strange desert

april 11ᵗʰ, 2020, 11:57 a.m. p.s.t.

social distance sing

serpentine thought mode
cruising across shifting sands
from shadow to light

april 11th, 2020, 12:01 p.m. p.s.t.

helios trots across
the sky past noon through evening
onward toward morning

april 11th, 2020, 12:05 p.m. p.s.t.

tomorrow churches
will celebrate christ's rebirth
and spread infection

april 11th, 2020, 12:29 p.m. p.s.t.

social distance sing

hot hungers of youth
cool as the long years stretch out
swim toward the sunset

april 11th, 2020, 2:43 p.m. p.s.t.

there once was a virus called corona
that caused many people to die alone a
tragedy completely
unsuited for a limerick...

april 12th, 2020, 3:23 a.m. p.s.t

there once was a man in quarantine
who wanted to go out and make the scene
which was problematic
for he was symptomatic
and there was not yet a vaccine

april 12th, 2020, 3:29 a.m. p.s.t

social distance sing

there once was a man who watched fox news
who held some poorly developed views
he said the virus was a hoax
bought himself a pack of smokes
and ignored dry coughs and other clues

april 12th, 2020, 3:29 a.m. p.s.t

sad story about
a nodding acquaintance
snatched from life too young

april 12th, 2020, 10:11 a.m. p.s.t

nodding acquaintance
seen in the cafes and bars
familiar stranger

april 12th, 2020, 10:15 a.m. p.s.t

social distance sing

sudden heart attack
pulled his car to side of road
died behind the wheel

april 12th, 2020, 10:24 a.m. p.s.t

as vonnegut wrote
"so it goes" "his peephole closed"
happens to us all

april 19th, 2020, 9:11 a.m. p.s.t.

it takes us death does
when it wants to death comes
and takes us that's all

april 12th, 2020, 10:30 a.m. p.s.t

social distance sing

death's gnomes come say
"follow us into the void"
body stays behind

april 12th, 2020, 10:33 a.m. p.s.t

one-hundred-thirteen-
thousand-three-hundred-twenty-nine
confirmed deaths to date

april 12th, 2020, 12:33 p.m. p.s.t.

lying tyrant move
threaten to fire doctors
who tell the truth

april 13th, 2020, 10:51 a.m. p.s.t.

68

social distance sing

one-hundred-eighteen-
thousand-three-hundred-sixty-two
confirmed deaths to date

april 13th, 2020, 10:54 a.m. p.s.t.

push a new lie
marketer-in-chief maneuver
bury the truth

april 13th, 2020, 10:57 a.m. p.s.t.

why expect sanity
in a world led by sociopaths
we're fools

april 13th, 2020, 11:03 a.m. p.s.t.

outrage fatigue
kakistocrats kleptocrats
pillage the nation

april 13th, 2020, 7:26 p.m. p.s.t.

ennui meets
revolutionary fervor
meets melancholy

april 13th, 2020, 9:13 p.m. p.s.t.

what is a virus
communication system
talking through humans

april 14th, 2020, 12:55 a.m. p.s.t.

social distance sing

minuscule parts
virus human galaxy
of something so grand

april 14th, 2020, 12:59 a.m. p.s.t.

space the final front
ear-nose-and-throat specialist
open wide say "ahhh"

april 14th, 2020, 1:01 a.m. p.s.t.

gutter puddle door
to enter reflected world
eyes see eyes see eyes

april 14th, 2020, 1:05 a.m. p.s.t.

alone beneath the electric lights
what if we could do without them
and learned to honor darkness
like our ancestors did
before they captured
fire to hold
in rock rings
in caves
awed

april 14th, 2020, 1:45 a.m. p.s.t.

in awe
our ancestors'
ancestors' ancestors
gazing at lightning in the sky
in awe

april 14th, 2020, 1:50 a.m. p.s.t.

social distance sing

we approach the sacred
like cats through tall grass
sneaking up to the pond
where the golden carp swim

april 14th, 2020, 1:54 a.m. p.s.t.

rainbow swirl of oil
on surface of street-water
lovely pollution

april 14th, 2020, 1:12 a.m. p.s.t.

virus
you've slowed the world
to a standstill and let
it breathe again for awhile
clear skies

april 14th, 2020, 1:12 a.m. p.s.t.

social distance sing

"the blind have no fear
of the darkness," said the mute
the deaf man nodded

april 14th, 2020, 4:21 a.m. p.s.t.

one-hundred-twenty-four-
thousand-nine-hundred-eighteen
confirmed deaths to date

april 14th, 2020, 10:36 a.m. p.s.t.

how many more jobs
lost how many evictions
how many senseless
bankruptcies from medical
debt before revolution

april 14th, 2020, 2:16 a.m. p.s.t.

74

social distance sing

revolution is
the bold lamb turning to face
the wolf gnashing at
its haunches to fight rather
than submit to certain death

april 14th, 2020, 2:20 a.m. p.s.t.

the lord was my wolf
the shepherd once used his dogs
to keep me in line
i slipped away in the night
and now the wolf is my lord

april 14th, 2020, 2:25 a.m. p.s.t.

a look at the news
liars fools and maniacs
beyond our control

april 15th, 2020, 1:47 p.m. p.s.t.

social distance sing

koyaanisqatsi
our lives are out of balance
our world is on the
verge of cataclysmic change
lunatics and fools in charge

april 15th, 2020, 1:52 p.m. p.s.t.

one-hundred-thirty-three-
thousand-eight-hundred-seventy-nine
confirmed deaths to date

april 15th, 2020, 2:09 p.m. p.s.t.

ghostly time shift vibe
reading dead rocker bio
tales of ancient grunge

april 16th, 2020, 12:18 a.m. p.s.t.

social distance sing

apropos of age
riffs from long-forgotten songs
discarded fashions
lipstick traces on spent butts
in history's cracked dustbin

april 16ᵗʰ, 2020, 1:03 a.m. p.s.t.

what's too recherche
for so-called "average readers"
commands attention
from lone seeker in the night
a campfire seen through dark woods

april 16ᵗʰ, 2020, 1:49 a.m. p.s.t.

one-hundred-forty-two-
thousand-seven-hundred-twelve
confirmed deaths to date

april 16ᵗʰ, 2020, 10:24 a.m. p.s.t.

77

social distance sing

headlights shine on waves
roar and shoosh of ebb and flow
drunk strangers dancing
in a parking lot at night
smash of dropped bottle laughter

april 16th, 2020, 2:03 a.m. p.s.t.

memories bleed like
purple burst of red meets blue
blue greened by yellow
wet paper watercolors
orange burst of yellowed red

april 16th, 2020, 2:09 a.m. p.s.t

last night's dream montage
fixing building and cleaning
old workplace settings
empty sense of wasted time
better days that might have been

april 16th, 2020, 10:32 a.m. p.s.t.

social distance sing

a sense of slow train-wreck underway
those of us in the caboose stunned
by tales of the engineer
his rank incompetence
and plain disregard
for social norms
keep us tense
fearing
doom

april 16th, 2020, 3:04 p.m. p.s.t.

one-hundred-forty-five
thousand-five-hundred-seventy-four
confirmed deaths to date

april 17th, 2020, p.m. p.s.t.

the man takes off his
virus-prevention mask to
smoke a cigarette

april 17th, 2020, 4:18 p.m. p.s.t.

social distance sing

current sidewalk scene
man in motorized wheelchair
zooms past guy on crutches

april 17th, 2020, 4:18 p.m. p.s.t.

one-hundred-fifty-nine-
thousand-six-hundred-twenty-one
confirmed deaths to date

april 18th, 2020, 2:36 p.m. p.s.t.

let's begin again
things have gone horribly wrong
crawl into the sea

april 19th, 2020, 12:21 a.m. p.s.t.

social distance sing

remembering a
perfect day i remember
forgetting the past

april 19th, 2020, 12:23 a.m. p.s.t.

sadness returns like
skies darkened by insect swarms
above drought-dried ponds

april 19th, 2020, 12:25 a.m. p.s.t.

who would you be if
you could choose to be anyone
me i'd pick me

april 19th, 2020, 12:27 a.m. p.s.t.

social distance sing

alone in my room
computer hums
refrigerator hums
i join in
i hum
hmmmmmmm

april 19th, 2020, 12:29 a.m. p.s.t.

alone in my mind
sort of but no for there are
so many of me

april 19th, 2020, 12:30 a.m. p.s.t.

what to do today
go to sleep we all agree
every one of me

april 19th, 2020, 12:31 a.m. p.s.t.

social distance sing

a real poet would
never _____
go ahead do it

april 19th, 2020, 12:33 a.m. p.s.t.

resist
that's what they say
but the damage is done
the tornado has trashed the town
rebuild

april 19th, 2020, 12:39 a.m. p.s.t.

this era we're in
mass graves for uninsured dead
world's richest country

april 19th, 2020, 8:23 a.m. p.s.t.

a big pile of amputated feet
in an old black-and-white photo
of a hospital tent from
a bloody civil war
battlefield conflict
returns to mind
saw it in
some old
book

april 19th, 2020, 1:06 a.m. p.s.t.

one-hundred-sixty-
two-thousand-five
confirmed deaths to date

april 19th, 2020, 8:45 a.m. p.s.t.

capitalism
has entered its death spiral
destroying what's for
the collective good of all
to coddle the overfed

april 19th, 2020, 8:52 a.m. p.s.t.

social distance sing

trump won't listen to the doc
lord please send us mr spock
we need logic
not hodgepodge sick
plans for turning back the clock

april 19th, 2020, 9:03 a.m. p.s.t.

there once was a raging narcissist
who needed to see a psychiatrist
he became president
and destroyed the government
despite the left's attempt to resist

april 19th, 2020, 9:11 a.m. p.s.t.

what's more likely to
drive one to commit suicide
love or lack of love

april 19th, 2020, 12:24 p.m. p.s.t.

social distance sing

more accurately
what's more likely to cause harm
bad love or no love

april 19th, 2020, 12:27 p.m. p.s.t.

people tend to leave
bad love out of the picture
it's a type of love

april 19th, 2020, 12:29 p.m. p.s.t.

people tend to talk
about the power of love
that it heals all wounds
they'll sing that it's all you need
what a load of crap

april 19th, 2020, 12:32 p.m. p.s.t.

social distance sing

hey love is great sure
but don't get carried away
it is what it is
but it ain't what it ain't too
it'll drive you nuts sometimes

april 19th, 2020, 12:35 p.m. p.s.t.

"love stinks yeah yeah" as
peter wolf of the j geil's
band sang way back when

april 24th, 2020, 3:11 p.m. p.s.t.

like alcohol
love is fine
so long as you don't
overdo it

april 19th, 2020, 12:37 p.m. p.s.t.

social distance sing

who sang "love is like
oxygen" I want to say
air supply ha-ha

april 24th, 2020, 3:14 p.m. p.s.t.

"love" gets used loosely
i love many sentences
in lew warsh's book
the origin of the world
but don't want to marry them

april 19th, 2020, 12:40 p.m. p.s.t.

i love the shape of
anglicized haiku its length
but i break its rules

april 19th, 2020, 12:43 p.m. p.s.t.

social distance sing

if haiku were my
wife she'd likely divorce me
for being unfaithful

april 19th, 2020, 12:47 p.m. p.s.t.

well as the kids say
i can't live by her rules man
i gotta be me

april 19th, 2020, 12:52 p.m. p.s.t.

i neglect to end
for one common example
with the word springtime

april 19th, 2020, 12:55 p.m. p.s.t.

worse i neglect to
mention a season at all
not even winter

april 19th, 2020, 4:16 p.m. p.s.t.

oh i could go on
about how bad a husband
i've been to haiku

april 19th, 2020, 12:59 p.m. p.s.t.

eyeing senryu
lasciviously at the bar
winking at tanka

april 19th, 2020, 1:03 p.m. p.s.t.

social distance sing

help us stop the virus' spread
stay indoors and flatten the curve
don't be a dumb-ass use your head
help us stop the virus' spread
so fewer people wind up dead
give doctors the hand they deserve
help them stop the virus' spread
stay indoors and flatten the curve

april 19th, 2020, 4:11 p.m. p.s.t.

bats this time not rats
through pangolins perhaps
camus i think of you

april 19th, 2020, 4:57 p.m. p.s.t.

precious poetry
has run its course has it not
bring it back to bone
muscle sinew guts and blood
down from your tower princess

april 19th, 2020, 5:02 p.m. p.s.t.

social distance sing

a life of the mind
without life of the body
to refer back to
is a swim through silver clouds
while silent empty bells swing

april 19th, 2020, 5:06 p.m. p.s.t.

one-hundred-sixty-eight-
thousand-nine-hundred-thirty-eight
confirmed deaths to date

april 20th, 2020, 11:47 a.m. p.s.t.

don't let the world hang
its definitions on you
define yourself

april 20th, 2020, 11:53 a.m. p.s.t.

social distance sing

one-hundred-seventy-five-
thousand-seven-hundred-fifty-nine
confirmed deaths to date

april 21st, 2020, 12:25 p.m. p.s.t.

there's nothing normal
about what we've called normal
go forward not back

april 21st, 2020, 4:17 p.m. p.s.t.

turn to sun and wind
oil belongs in the ground
future of clear skies

april 21st, 2020, 4:20 p.m. p.s.t.

social distance sing

we must slow down
human hyper-mania
is killing the earth

april 21st, 2020, 4:26 p.m. p.s.t.

why are we here
this "vale of soul-making" now
seems a tragic farce

april 21st, 2020, 4:28 p.m. p.s.t.

yes a tragic farce
or farcical tragedy
plainly a shitshow

april 21st, 2020, 4:29 p.m. p.s.t.

social distance sing

black shapes cross gray clouds
three crows harass an eagle
sky-high shadow play

april 21st, 2020, 4:31 p.m. p.s.t.

the urban hermit
gazes out fourth floor window
at the world below
quiet foggy gray morning
another day to explore

april 22nd, 2020, a.m. p.s.t.

aches and pains of age
closing in on six decades
what's been accomplished
mountains of ink-scrawled papers
songs sung only to himself

april 22nd, 2020, a.m. p.s.t.

95

social distance sing

thoughts of the people
friends enemies frenemies
he's known through the years
and the buildings he's lived in
the streets cafes and barrooms

april 22nd, 2020, a.m. p.s.t.

dead relatives who
visit now only in dreams
former co-workers
friends not seen in many years
memories of youthful days

april 22nd, 2020, a.m. p.s.t.

scenes he drifted through
some where he stayed put awhile
the energy fields
of human conversation
like prairie dog villages

april 22nd, 2020, a.m. p.s.t.

social distance sing

heads pop out of holes
yip-yip-yipping the day's gossip
saw them on a trip
badlands of south dakota
four long decades ago

april 22nd, 2020, a.m. p.s.t.

he goes poeming
like fishing with his grandpa
when he was a boy
bait the hook drop the line
sinker hits bottom now wait

april 22nd, 2020, a.m. p.s.t.

one has lucky days
and/or not-so-lucky days
some days the fish bite
some days only the flies bite
and you scratch your sun-tanned skin

april 22nd, 2020, a.m. p.s.t.

social distance sing

some fishermen dream
of catching the biggest fish
that's ever been caught
while others are there to
catch dinner for their families

april 22nd, 2020, a.m. p.s.t.

so the question begs
are you a giant dead fish
stuffed shellacked and hung
on the wall behind your desk
poet or a plate of food

april 22nd, 2020, a.m. p.s.t.

does that even work
analogies are funny
they can get stupid
the sea is a street of skies
the sky is a street of seas

april 22nd, 2020, a.m. p.s.t.

social distance sing

good morning hello
my back aches and my breath stinks
aren't you glad you're
not here to hear me complain
water boiling for coffee

april 22nd, 2020, a.m. p.s.t.

grandiosity
can be an impediment
to finding one's way
humility is better
get over yourself and write

april 22nd, 2020, a.m. p.s.t.

get over yourself
you're a big bag of water
oh there's more to it
yeah sure it's complicated
no actually it's simple

april 22nd, 2020, a.m. p.s.t.

social distance sing

we're bags of water
all life on earth is one sea
though separated
somewhat into different bags
swimming walking flying bags

april 22nd, 2020, a.m. p.s.t.

we're bags of water
building nuclear weapons
so we can blow up
other big bags of water
so they won't blow us up first

april 22nd, 2020, a.m. p.s.t.

we're bags of water
in an age of pandemic
led by a buffoon
with a team of lying thieves
who ignore doctors' orders

april 22nd, 2020, a.m. p.s.t.

social distance sing

we're bags of water
with heads full of hopes and dreams
spouting thoughts and prayers
to loved ones of the murdered
while backing the n r a

april 22nd, 2020, a.m. p.s.t.

we're bags of water
driven mad with lust and greed
longing for glory
who'll kill to get a medal
who'll die for a rich man's lie

april 22nd, 2020, a.m. p.s.t.

we're bags of water
full of pretense and put-on
posturing scenesters
performing "i'm a poet"
more so than writing poems

april 22nd, 2020, a.m. p.s.t.

we're bags of water
we're just big bags of water
we're bags of water
we're just big bags of water
we're just big bags of water

april 22nd, 2020, a.m. p.s.t.

grandiosity
can be an impediment
remember that you
are a big bag of water
humility is better

april 22nd, 2020, 8:51 a.m. p.s.t.

One-hundred-eighty-
thousand-five-hundred-seventy-eight
confirmed deaths to date

april 22nd, 2020, 9:22 a.m. p.s.t.

social distance sing

can't recall who wrote
"the world is too much with us"
probably ernie
but holy hell yeah no shit
just glanced at my facebook feed

april 22nd, 2020, 9:23 a.m. p.s.t.

the internet is
like a bucket of sorrow
we dump on our heads
each morning and each evening
to soak ourselves in sadness

april 22nd, 2020, 9:25 a.m. p.s.t.

the greediest pricks
are in charge of everything
the world's in ruins
the virus is still spreading
the climate is collapsing

april 22nd, 2020, 9:29 a.m. p.s.t.

social distance sing

thanks internet for
reminding me of problems
beyond my control
am I exaggerating
a little but not a lot

april 22nd, 2020, 9:33 a.m. p.s.t.

wars and pandemic
dangerous leadership then
a cat video
an old poem by du fu
to put things in perspective

april 22nd, 2020, 9:39 a.m. p.s.t.

"same as it ever was"
as david byrne sings in that
talking heads' song
the rolling blunder rolls on
life's rich pageant one long folly

april 22nd, 2020, 9:52 a.m. p.s.t.

one-hundred-eighty-five-
thousand-five-hundred-four
confirmed deaths to date

april 23rd, 2020, a.m. p.s.t.

how will the wealthy
make use of this pandemic
to increase their wealth

april 23rd, 2020, a.m. p.s.t.

how will the powerful
make use of this pandemic
to increase power

april 23rd, 2020, a.m. p.s.t.

social distance sing

let me count the ways
actually i'd rather not
sharks were made to eat

april 23rd, 2020, a.m. p.s.t.

exploited workers
underpaid and uninsured
feed the idle rich

april 23rd, 2020, a.m. p.s.t.

breathing fast and hard
while lying perfectly still
was that the virus

april 23rd, 2020, a.m. p.s.t.

lifetime spent planning
hopes for a better future
that never arrived

april 23rd, 2020, p.m. p.s.t.

"creative" equals
"wrong" to the rule followers
out to please the boss
bound to serve authority
blind to possibility

april 23rd, 2020, p.m. p.s.t.

i feel the ghost of
an old poem in the lines
of one i've written
perhaps i even stole it
if so ancient bard thank you

april 23rd, 2020, p.m. p.s.t.

social distance sing

sometimes people are like
"be my significant other"
and i'm like "nah"

april 23rd, 2020, p.m. p.s.t.

peaceful quiet day
insignificance is bliss
reading and writing

april 23rd, 2020, p.m. p.s.t.

online solitaire
i remember playing cards
my grandmother's hands

april 23rd, 2020, 10:01 p.m. p.s.t.

social distance sing

my grandma's hands and
bill withers' "grandma's hands" and
prine's "hello in there"

april 24th, 2020, early a.m. p.s.t.

our backward nation
run by fools and criminals
god bless um a wreck

april 24th, 2020, early a.m. p.s.t.

corporate bailouts but
states should declare bankruptcy
a kleptocracy

april 24th, 2020, early a.m. p.s.t.

social distance sing

his teeth
keep falling out
and his eyes keep bleeding
you think he should be president
really

april 24th, 2020, early a.m. p.s.t.

our backward nation
is being looted daily
thieving kleptocrats

april 24th, 2020, early a.m. p.s.t.

animal passion
in the tangled underbrush
beneath our costumes

april 24th, 2020, early a.m. p.s.t.

social distance sing

in isolation
one must argue with oneself
no one else to blame

april 24th, 2020, early a.m. p.s.t.

washington d c
billionaire ventriloquists
hands up the backs of
these political dummies
choosing words moving their mouths

april 24th, 2020, early a.m. p.s.t.

"the earth died screaming"
while the great Tom Waits lay dreaming
that song may come true

april 24th, 2020, 4:01 p.m. p.s.t.

social distance sing

such delusional
arrogant apes all of us
self-killing species

april 24th, 2020, 4:05 p.m. p.s.t.

one-hundred-ninety-six-
thousand-nine-hundred-forty-eight
confirmed deaths to date

april 24th, 2020, 4:12 p.m. p.s.t.

what is this life for
spend much time asking that
never an answer

april 25th, 2020, a.m. p.s.t.

social distance sing

talking to myself
one human among billions
in this mystery

april 25th, 2020, a.m. p.s.t.

here's a phrase i like
genuflecting gizzard snark
it's not too useful

april 25th, 2020, a.m. p.s.t.

here's a phrase i like
heliotropic flirt brigade
it's not too useful

april 25th, 2020, a.m. p.s.t.

here's a phrase i like
sonogram ski patrol shark
it's not too useful

april 25th, 2020, a.m. p.s.t.

here's a phrase i like
pink carbona poodle mermaid
it's not too useful

april 25th, 2020, a.m. p.s.t.

time for an edit
this has become a kids' book
cut out the curses

april 25th, 2020, a.m. p.s.t.

this book needs a plot
character development
and epiphanies

april 25th, 2020, a.m. p.s.t.

first there was novel
coronavirus
now there's coronavirus
the novel soon to be
a major motion picture

april 25th, 2020, a.m. p.s.t.

two-hundred-one-
thousand-seven-hundred-forty-three
confirmed deaths to date

april 25th, 2020, a.m. p.s.t.

social distance sing

gray skies and moisture
avoid news of outside world
a cool spring morning

april 25th, 2020, a.m. p.s.t.

enjoyment of life
the most basic pleasure of
simply being here

april 25th, 2020, a.m. p.s.t.

close your eyes and breathe
drink a glass of cool water
look smell listen taste

april 25th, 2020, a.m. p.s.t.

social distance sing

striving frustrated
we tangle ourselves in knots
untangle relax

april 25th, 2020, a.m. p.s.t.

it's tough to stop though
stop rocking death comes knocking
capitalist treadmill

april 25th, 2020, a.m. p.s.t.

worker's hamster wheel
run run run and get a treat
step off wheel and starve

april 25th, 2020, a.m. p.s.t.

they want you hungry
executives stockholders
they want you frightened

april 25th, 2020, a.m. p.s.t.

manipulating
human resources is key
to making profits

april 25th, 2020, a.m. p.s.t.

cruel stupid system
what a way to run a world
time for transformation

april 25th, 2020, a.m. p.s.t.

social distance sing

life in one small room
my mind travels far and wide
body just sits here

april 25th, 2020, p.m. p.s.t.

imagination
swim through the sky to the moon
have a picnic there

april 25th, 2020, p.m. p.s.t.

can you imagine
life in true democracy
with sane president

april 25th, 2020, p.m. p.s.t.

119

social distance sing

can you imagine
a compassionate nation
with wise leadership

april 25th, 2020, p.m. p.s.t.

can you imagine
respect for working people
livable wages

april 25th, 2020, p.m. p.s.t.

can you imagine
access to healthcare for all
human dignity

april 25th, 2020, p.m. p.s.t.

can you imagine
free higher education
student debt relief

april 25ᵗʰ, 2020, p.m. p.s.t.

can you imagine
leadership dedicated
to conserving earth

april 25ᵗʰ, 2020, p.m. p.s.t.

can you imagine
wise stewardship of resources
not pillaging

april 25ᵗʰ, 2020, p.m. p.s.t.

social distance sing

content as a child
with new crayons and paper
i sit here and write

april 25th, 2020, p.m. p.s.t.

the world is a mess
i feel right at home because
my life is a mess

april 25th, 2020, p.m. p.s.t.

seattle morning
grey clouds soft drizzle slight breeze
crow lands on roof

april 25th, 2020, p.m. p.s.t.

social distance sing

pink flowering tree
all dressed up for birds and bees
hey boys over here

april 25th, 2020, p.m. p.s.t.

accumulation
of details reveals a world
in a book's pages

april 25th, 2020, p.m. p.s.t.

aging hippic is
a less embarrassing look than
aging punk rocker
thought the aging long-haired man
who was wearing a tie-dye

april 25th, 2020, p.m. p.s.t.

social distance sing

the squall of voices
in the twitterverse era
can be unnerving

april 25th, 2020, p.m. p.s.t.

shhh sit still be calm
no need to react again
let it flow past you

april 25th, 2020, p.m. p.s.t.

everywhere we see
fault-finders rushing judgment
breathe sit still stare

april 25th, 2020, p.m. p.s.t.

social distance sing

blue sky afternoon
clouds you could dollop onto
hot cocoa and drink

april 25th, 2020, p.m. p.s.t.

my grandparents' house
an old friend of theirs saying
she'd like to ride clouds
after she died and look down
on the goings-on of earth

april 25th, 2020, p.m. p.s.t.

many years later
the memory arrives and
I look to the sky
hello up there old woman
cloud surfer extraordinaire

april 25th, 2020, p.m. p.s.t.

125

social distance sing

life is a long tube
some of us are digested
faster than others

april 25th, 2020, p.m. p.s.t.

feeling grandiose
get over it   we're just turds
in a huge worm's guts

april 25th, 2020, p.m. p.s.t.

life is one long room
enter walk through and exit
don't forget to dance

april 25th, 2020, p.m. p.s.t.

social distance sing

many shades of green
against the grey and white clouds
treetops of springtime

april 25th, 2020, p.m. p.s.t.

what kind of future
for generations to come
a barren hellscape
or utopian garden
planet of coexistence

april 25th, 2020, p.m. p.s.t.

these shapes and patterns
letters arranged on the page
a mystery we
take for granted this language
some say it is a virus

april 25th, 2020, p.m. p.s.t.

social distance sing

the black dogs arrive
and leap against the white door
of the old red house
the sun sets behind the hills
and the yellow moon rises

april 25th, 2020, p.m. p.s.t.

an old man stares back
the face of death in winter
he holds a red rose
between his stiffened blue lips
turn around   go back   go back

april 25th, 2020, p.m. p.s.t.

sit on the gray roof
contemplate the cracked white skull
found near the river
where the deer come down to drink
when the world grows cool at dusk

april 25th, 2020, p.m. p.s.t.

social distance sing

write a little line
a snapshot of the moment
as it slips away

april 25th, 2020, p.m. p.s.t.

"time keeps on slipping"
as steve miller pointed out
"into the future"

april 25th, 2020, p.m. p.s.t.

everyone of us
as eddie vedder sings are
"runnin' out of sand"

april 25th, 2020, p.m. p.s.t.

129

social distance sing

you can't get lost if
you don't care where you're going
relax you're on earth

april 25th, 2020, p.m. p.s.t.

smooth off your handles
round yourself ungraspable
become hard to hold

april 25th, 2020, p.m. p.s.t.

the voracious need
for action and excitement
is destroying us
so many cartoon people
so many soft melting minds

april 25th, 2020, p.m. p.s.t.

130

social distance sing

write something boring
because it's funny sometimes
let yourself be dull
pursuit of profundity
is its own sort of boring

april 25th, 2020, p.m. p.s.t.

alone on the couch
an old man wearing sweatpants
decides he should write
something boring and succeeds
beginning "alone on the..."

april 25th, 2020, p.m. p.s.t.

properly expressed
boredom can be engaging
see for example
jim's journal by scott dikkers
boredom's part of life embrace it

april 25th, 2020, p.m. p.s.t.

social distance sing

tumultuous life
relax and enjoy yourself
as much as you can

april 25th, 2020, p.m. p.s.t.

close your eyes and breathe
separate inside from out
allow yourself joy

april 25th, 2020, p.m. p.s.t.

open the curtains
who is the director of
your internal film

april 25th, 2020, p.m. p.s.t.

social distance sing

the traffic outside
is a rushing river if
you want it to be

april 25th, 2020, p.m. p.s.t.

strange world of wonders
helicopter overhead
man in metal bug

april 25th, 2020, p.m. p.s.t.

sudden frenzy of crows
large and small   old and young
spring flying lessons

april 25th, 2020, p.m. p.s.t.

our orange clown king
manipulator-in-chief
plays the media
day after day after day
grifting gullible patsies

april 25th, 2020, p.m. p.s.t.

in the beginning
was followed by the middle
and then came the end

april 25th, 2020, p.m. p.s.t.

the beginning was
the end of the previous
beginning's middle

april 25th, 2020, p.m. p.s.t.

social distance sing

and so it goes
around and around
ouroboric

april 25th, 2020, p.m. p.s.t.

two-hundred-five-
thousand-nine-hundred-twenty-eight
confirmed deaths to date

april 26th, 2020, 10:19 a.m. p.s.t.

peace   morning coffee
let the day unfurl slowly
a sail catching wind

april 26th, 2020, a.m. p.s.t.

social distance sing

uncertain era
lone walker on a grey road
here comes the cool rain

april 26th, 2020, a.m. p.s.t.

we are all sick
in this toxic society
stimulus addicts

april 26th, 2020, a.m. p.s.t.

sit perfectly still
free and easy medicine
don't react just sit

april 26th, 2020, a.m. p.s.t.

social distance sing

what must I do now
nothing   not a fucking thing
just sit here   just sit

april 26th, 2020, a.m. p.s.t.

not here to squabble
rain falls and the river flows
let the mad birds squawk

april 26th, 2020, a.m. p.s.t.

the distant mountain
invisible destiny
grey clouds release rain

april 26th, 2020, a.m. p.s.t.

social distance sing

grey clouds drift away
destiny revealed anew
the distant mountain

april 26th, 2020, a.m. p.s.t.

we saw mount rainier
men came and built a building
to hide it from us

april 26th, 2020, a.m. p.s.t.

keep out keep in no
fences were made for jumping
young explorers seek

april 26th, 2020, a.m. p.s.t.

structures of guidance
and structures of confinement
one big sad prison

april 26th, 2020, a.m. p.s.t.

The silent noise of
invisible destiny
fields of energy

april 26th, 2020, a.m. p.s.t.

the part of us that
is part of the universe
that we are part of

april 26th, 2020, a.m. p.s.t.

morning thoughts about
invisible destiny's
mystery agents

april 26th, 2020, a.m. p.s.t.

the ebb and flow of
invisible destiny
the ocean of soul

april 26th, 2020, a.m. p.s.t.

seeking alignment
with ordinary magic's
mystery agents

april 26th, 2020, a.m. p.s.t.

social distance sing

mystery agents of
invisible destiny
guide us forward

april 26th, 2020, a.m. p.s.t.

silent unseen foe
virus in old folks' home
a soft deadly breeze

april 26th, 2020, a.m. p.s.t.

we are one being
gaia how do we heal you
followers must lead

april 26th, 2020, a.m. p.s.t.

social distance sing

a walk by the lake
mountains hidden behind clouds
ducklings in a row

april 26^{*th*}*, 2020, a.m. p.s.t.*

scolding with a squawk
black crow atop grey light post
keeping watch on us

april 26^{*th*}*, 2020, a.m. p.s.t.*

wearing a red dress
the woman walks her white dog
on a cool grey day

april 26^{*th*}*, 2020, a.m. p.s.t.*

social distance sing

man in a white mask
walks past man in a black mask
there is no gunfight

april 26th, 2020, a.m. p.s.t.

not masks
upper face exposed
more like muzzles

april 26th, 2020, a.m. p.s.t.

spy vs. spy
mad magazine
1972

april 26th, 2020, a.m. p.s.t.

social distance sing

reality is
imaginary he said
imagine that

april 26th, 2020, a.m. p.s.t.

old tools on the wall
hung as decorations now
once so useful

april 26th, 2020, a.m. p.s.t.

no animals were nocturnal
before humans went insane
with technology and war
can't prove it
just a theory

april 26th, 2020, a.m. p.s.t.

social distance sing

two-hundred-nine-
thousand-seven-hundred-twenty-nine
confirmed deaths to date

april 27th, 2020, 11:08 a.m. p.s.t.

how long before we
evolve beyond human form
we are primitive
forebears of some new beings
who'll look back on us with wonder

april 27th, 2020, 9:45 p.m. p.s.t.

Vascular terror possibilities are
In the air quite literally now.
Republicans want workers back to work
Under any circumstances.
Screw that!

april 27th, 2020, a.m. p.s.t.

social distance sing

Vague sense of dread palpable
In these uncertain times.
Risk-averse people wisely avoid crowds.
Uncertainty about the future is
Seriously bumming folks out right now.

april 27th, 2020, a.m. p.s.t.

two-hundred-fifteen-
thousand-two-hundred-thirty-one
confirmed deaths to date

april 28th, 2020, 11:51 a.m. p.s.t.

resourceful old crow
holds a stick in its beak
flying past my window

april 28th, 2020, 12:11 p.m. p.s.t.

social distance sing

nodding off on couch
slip into dreams climb back out
in two worlds at once

april 28th, 2020, 7:17 p.m. p.s.t.

a simple statement
that's expressed elegantly
clear blue sky above

april 29th, 2020, 8:44 a.m. p.s.t.

a clear mind at peace
moving through the world with ease
the flowing river

april 29th, 2020, 8:47 a.m. p.s.t.

a life of study
trail of words through the forest
the distant mountain

april 29th, 2020, 8:51 a.m. p.s.t.

two-hundred-twenty-
thousand-three-hundred-twenty-four
confirmed deaths to date

april 29th, 2020, 9:19 a.m. p.s.t.

clown on the king's throne
out-of-balance world shaken
oncoming chaos

april 30h, 2020, a.m. p.s.t.

social distance sing

people's needs ignored
handouts to the super-rich
children's food taken

april 30ʰ, 2020, a.m. p.s.t.

kids locked in cages
families separated
children kidnapped

april 30ʰ, 2020, a.m. p.s.t.

this is our true face
no more masks america
land of trail of tears
mirror mirror build a wall
who's the vainest of them all

april 30ʰ, 2020, a.m. p.s.t.

the poorly-informed
believe they're being oppressed
by the well-informed

april 30ʰ, 2020, 7:02 p.m. p.s.t.

protesters with guns
storm michigan's capitol
like cartoon people

april 30ʰ, 2020, 7:05 .m. p.s.t.

sick america
increasingly paranoid
beast pacing in cage

april 30ʰ, 2020, 7:20 p.m. p.s.t.

150

social distance sing

what'll make it stop
a biden presidency
ha-ha   ha-ha-ha

april 30ʰ, 2020, 7: 27 p.m. p.s.t.

my prescription
read more science articles
fewer qanon posts

april 30ʰ, 2020, 7:30 p.m. p.s.t.

what choice do we have
stick with hi-cal evil or
back to evil lite
politics – a puppet show
let it go   let your life flow

april 30ʰ, 2020, 7:36 p.m. p.s.t.

social distance sing

the flowing river
runs from the distant mountain
to the ancient sea
all things in their place and time
this human moment shall pass

april 30ʰ, 2020, 10:39 p.m. p.s.t.

the distant mountain
shall be worn away to sand
for all things must pass
even rivers will run dry
and alas the ancient sea

april 30ʰ, 2020, 10: 42 p.m. p.s.t.

two-hundred-thirty-three-
thousand-eight-hundred-twenty-four
confirmed deaths to date

april 30ᵗʰ, 2020, 11:35 p.m. p.s.t.

social distance sing

ah the cruelest month
national poetry month
nears its final tick

april 30ʰ, 2020, 11:51 p.m. p.s.t.

tock there it is now
the cruelest month has ended
so too has this book

may 1ˢᵗ, 2020, 12:02 a.m. p.s.t.

Steve Potter is a self-described multi-modal free-range poet more interested in exploring a broad range of possibilities old and new than in settling for long on any particular aesthetic stance.

His work has appeared in extant publications such as *Able Muse, Blazevox, E·Ratio, Otoliths, Marginalia, Word/For Word* as well as defunct and sorely missed publications such as *Arson, Pindeldyboz, Point No Point, The Temple,* and *3rd Bed.*

He received his MA from Queens College, CUNY which he attended nights while driving a plumbing supply delivery truck around New York City and Long Island by day. Born and raised on the south shore of Long Island, he has lived for most of the past twenty-five years in Seattle, Washington.

Potter writes and blogs about books and literature at bookfreak.us

stevepotterwrites@gmail.com

Lightning Source UK Ltd.
Milton Keynes UK
UKHW010812280620
365674UK00007B/142